BILLIARDS
RULE BOOK
2009

Edited & Compiled By:

Anoop Jain

SPORTS PUBLICATION

7/26, Ground Floor, Ansari Road,
Darya Ganj, New Delhi-110002
Phones: (Office) 65749511 (Fax) 011-23240261
(Mobile) 9868028838 (Residence) 27562163
E-mail: lakshaythani@hotmail.com

Published by:

SPORTS PUBLICATION
7/26, Ground Floor, Ansari Road, Darya Ganj, New Delhi-1100◄
Ph. : (Office) 65749511, 23240261 (Mobile) 9868028838
      (Residence) 27562163 (Fax) 011-23240261
E-mail: *lakshaythani@hotmail.com*

© 2009 Publishers

I.S.B.N: 81-7879-134-X

PRINTED IN INDIA 2009

Laser Typeset by:
JAIN MEDIA GRAPHICS,
C-4/95-A, Keshav Puram, Delhi-35

Printed by:
CHAWLA OFFSET PRINTERS, Delhi-110052

Price: Rs. 140/-

CONTENTS

1

INTRODUCTION

The earliest recorded mention of billiards was in France in 1429 and Louis XI, King of France 1461-83, is reported to have had a billiard table. The first tournament at this style of play was held in New York from November 14th to 26th, 1881, and was won by Joseph Dion in a field of ten players. This version of the game enjoyed considerable popularity before it too passed from the scene.

Billiards is a fascinating game which one can play for hours together within the precincts of one's own home or in a club. It is fascinating because it puts to a severe test, your sense of precision of eye and the control of your mind. The atmosphere in which you play is uniquely peaceful and relaxing.

2

TECHNIQUES AND SKILLS OF BILLIARDS & SNOOKERS

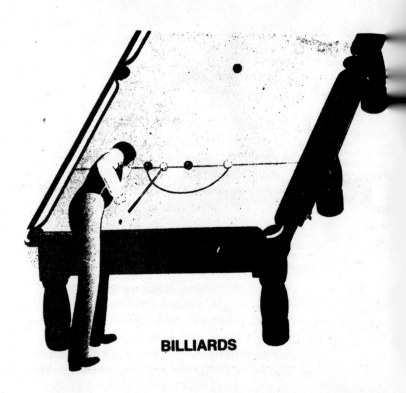

BILLIARDS

Billions of people in many countries are now snooker-playing regulars, yet only a very small percentage are able to play to the kind of high standard where a century break is within their capabilities. For most of the game's underachievers, the reason lies in a lack of practice, the misapplication of basic principles, or a combination of both. As with bad cueing habits, an awkward stance or a weak bridge is difficult to rectify, and it does not take a genuius to work out the paramount importance of concentrating on getting the basics right from the very start.

THE BRIDGE

While idiosyncrasies exist with the grips and stances of different players, the bridge is usually the same. The role of the bridge is twofold. It helps you deliver the cue and, acting as the front part of a tripod - the other two parts being the player's legs - it gives a stance greater stability.

THE STANCE

Unless you stand in the correct manner and also deliver the cue through the ball correctly, you will find it difficult to progress, regardless of how many practice hours you put in. Of the professionals its seen, which is most, it would have to say Australia's John Campbell, who is 6ft 4in tall, has easily the widest stance.

THE GRIP

The last, but most certainly not least important, of the three basics is the grip. There are different grips, and asked such questions as, 'Where do it is hole the cue?' or 'How tightly do need to grip it?' Personally, it's hold the cue around an inch from the butt for long shots and around three inches from the butt when it is in close, because that gives me more 'feel' - and not too tightly. If you grip the cue too strongly you are undoubtedly susceptible to 'snatching' in pressure situations.

It believe a looser, fluid grip like mine enables a player to cue with rhythm, tempo and above all else consistency.

On the other hand, it does not pay to hold the cue too lightly. With the modern game requiring a player to complete a whole range of power shots, such as deep screws and stuns, some strength in the grip is needed.

To retain fluency and reduce tension in the cue-arm the grip of one, two or sometimes three fingers is relaxed from the cue during the backswing and is reapplied as the cue is being propelled towards the cue-ball. Novices need not be unduly concerned about these advanced shots, but even they can benefit by realising the importance of finding the right balance between the fierce and loose extremes of grip. As with most things on the technical side of snooker, a player needs to search for a suitable compromise.

Conclusion

BRIDGE

(i) Raise the knuckles above the surface of the table and cock thumb high to form a channel for the cue to run through.

(ii) Spread your fingers as wide as possible without making it uncomfortable.

STANCE

(i) Your weight should be distributed so that the only movement during the shot is made by the cue-arm.

(ii) Your feet should not be too close together or, indeed, too far apart.

GRIP

(i) It is important to keep your wrist flexible but firm.

(ii) Hold the cue a couple of inches from the butt and not too tightly.

BILLIARDS RULE BOOK

SETS AND PLANTS

Television commentators have fallen into the habit of describing two slightly different types of shot under the umbrella term 'plant'. Strictly speaking, a plant is a position in which it is possible to play one object ball on to another in such away that the second object ball will be potted. Obviously this can apply only to reds except in free ball situations and it really applies only to positions in which a player would actively consider taking on such a shot.

Sets

The typical set is a situation in which two reds are directly in line with a pocket. It is often assumed that such a pot is unmissable—that it is, in fact, a gift shot. If ever they miss them, players assume that they were wrong in their original assessment of the situation, that the balls were not in fact in line with the pocket. In this they are more than likely to be wrong.

The 'Squeeze' Effect

The term usually applied to this phenomenon is 'squeeze'. The force imparted to the first red by the cue ball, being off the potting line, is said to have the effect of squeezing the second red so that it comes off at a slightly different angle and therefore off the potting line. If the two reds are close to the pocket your error will go unpunished. The further they are from the pocket, and the slower you play the shot, the greater the deviation from the potting line.

Plants

If the two object balls are not touching, the set becomes a plant. The easiest plants re those in which the two reds are very close together, and both directly in line with the pocket, like a natural set. The further the reds are apart, and the further they are from the pocket, the more difficult the plant. In either case, the principle for playing this successfully is the same.

Judging the Angle

To judge the angle, you should address the first red as though it were the cue ball, and then try to carry the mental image of the two reds in line with the pocket with you as you return to the cue ball to select your angle. Plants are delightfully satisfying shots to bring off successfully, but initially you should resist the temptation to be very ambitious with them. There is every danger of leaving a ball 'on' if you miss, and where feasible you should consider playing them as shots to nothing'.

Trick Shots

Trick shots have nothing to do with snooker proper, but occasional televised displays of them have proved immensely popular. Generally speaking, trick shot routines are featured at the end of exhibition evenings or when a one-sided match has ended long before the anticipated time.

DOUBLING THE BALL

Novices tend to enjoy playing doubles, whereas professionals are chary of them. The reason for this is simple enough. The novice is not really expecting to bring the shot off, and when he not infrequently does it looks and feels a spectacular shot particularly if he has really cracked it in. The professional has no interest in spectacular looking shots.

Trial and Error

As with potting angles, the only way you will learn to make doubles is through trial and error, and by careful observation of what happens when you attempt them from various positions. Sometimes it helps to go to the intended pocket and, imagine the shot backwards. One marginal advantage the double has over normal shots is that once you have settled on the angle, you can give over your entire concentration to cue ball control.

The Cocked-hat Double

This could be properly described as a treble, since it involves playing the object ball off three cushions into a middle pocket. It may strike you as fanciful that you could succeed with such a shot other than by luck, but it is not as difficult as it appears. Unlike the corner pocket, the middle pocket is comparatively open. Moreover, if you miss it, the object ball with run free of the pocket, assuming you have played the shot with reasonable strength.

THE UNMISSABLE PLANT

If you can deliver the cue even halfway straight you will make this shot firs time. As near as anything ever is, it can be described as unmissable. Place the blue on its spot, with a red touching it in direct line with the pink and black spots. Place the cue ball on the brown spot.

Zigzag

This is the most difficult so far described because it is a power shot using side, but it is worth persevering with because the effect is spectacular. Place the eleven reds and black as indicated, and the cue ball near the green spot. Play a poer shot with moderate screw and right-hand side, aiming for the cushion where first red, cannon off the red back on to the cushion, then on to the second red, then the cushion and so on down the line, until the cue ball finally pots the black.

Black in the middle

This is not unmissable means difficult. Like so many trick shots it is a cunning plant that at first sight looks impossible. The three reds and the black are all touching, and all firmly on the cushion. The fourth red is a quarter of an inch from the touching group, and a half a ball's width from the cushion. The fifth is a ball's width out from the middle pocket. Play the cue ball medium strength with plenty of screw.

The Snake

This plant on the black employs all fifteen reds, and it is as easy to play off as it is exhilarating to view. Place the balls as indicated, about three inches apart with the final red and the black directly in line with the pocket. This is a power shot, played full on the first red, plain ball.

3

RULES OF BILLIARDS & SNOOKERS

THE GAME

In a game either 2 players can compete or 4. Different kinds of balls are used in the game which can be of white, spotted, plain, and red colour. In-offs, pots and cannons are also used in the game. Strokes are awarded with points while fouls is penalised by deduction. After a specified period of time points scored by each player will be valued and player with more points will be declare winner.

<u>Starting of Game</u>

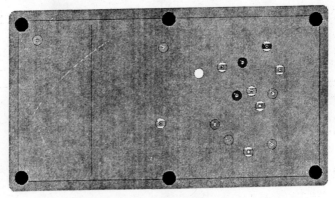

i. At beginning of game red should be placed on **spot, the** first player plays from in-hand and the game **starts with** first stroke;

ii. The choice of ball, order of play, if not agreed upon, should be decided by stringing, the winner having the option, and should remain unaffected throughout the game.

Details of Scoring

In below mentioned way points should be awarded:

i. For a pot red and in-off red—3 points;

ii. When in-off is combined with a cannon—2 or 3 points;

iii. For a cannon, pot white and in-off white—2 points;

Order of Play

Players will play turn by turn till no score is made by striker.

To Play from In-hand

Cue-ball should:

a. Before hitting any ball in baulk it should hit a ball or cushion out of baulk;

b. Be played out of baulk

Limitation of Cannons

Not in conjunction with hazard, 75 consecutive cannons are permissible in game. Referee is required to inform the striker after expiry of 70 cannons.

Penalty

Player committing any of the following fouls can be penalised with forfeiture of his points as well as his turn:

i. if any player strike a moving cue ball or an object ball;

ii. Player who does not put his either foot on floor while executing the stroke;

iii. Any player who touch or disturb the cue ball or any object ball;

iv. If cue ball goes into pocket;

v. Jumping cue ball of table.

Other than Striker someone other striking the ball

If ball is strucked by anybody other than striker, referee should put the ball again at its place so that striker can strike it.

Play without Disturbance

(1) Striker should call the number of ball which he wants to pocket. If ball he called has already pocketed, he should be provided with any other ball. Other balls pocketed on same stroke should be ignored which should be spotted again if called ball has not pocketed.

(2) Ball which rolls up on a rail but come back to table should be considered to be in play.

(3) Object ball should be spotted if cue ball is in hand and object ball is within the head string. Ball nearer to head string should be spotted if within head string there are more than 1 object ball.

(4) Each player's turn is known as an inning, thus play is conducted in innings. As long as a player legally pockets a ball on each stroke, inning should remain continue. Opponent becomes shooter in case striker failed to legally pocket a ball or committed any foul.

(5) Ball which have been striken by anybody other than striker should be replaced at table at its original place.

(6) It is an error that a called ball jumps the table. For this error a player has to give up his inning.

Restrictions of Hazards

Consecutive hazards, being not in conjunction with a cannon are restricted to 15.

After 10 hazards referee will inform the striker.

In by a single stroke more than 1 hazard is made it should be counted as 1 but all points should be considered to have scored.

The non-striker's ball should be off the table and spotted after 15-hazard on middle spot of D, as a consequence of striker's last stroke.

Miss

i. In condition other than the following miss should be considered a foul:

When striker is in hand and there is no ball out of baulk;

ii. Miss should be penalised with 2 points.

Ball on the Edge of Pocket

i. Ball which falls into pocket without hitting other ball should be replaced.

ii. If ball which have been striked out by striker hit the ball on edge of pocket, all balls should be replaced and striker should strike again.

iii. Ball which balances momentarily on the edge and falls in should be replaced.

Balls Touching

If striker's ball is touching non-striker's ball, it should be placed on centre spot. If striker's ball is touching anyother ball, red should be placed on the spot.

Fouls

Following procedure should be followed if a foul takes place:

i. Refree should state loudly Foul.

ii. if it is not awarded by umpire or claimed by other player, before making of next stroke it should be ignored.

iii. Ball which have been spotted improperly should remain at place where situates.

iv. All points scored before awarding of foul should be taken into consideration.

Benefit of penalty of a player is enjoyed by his opponent. For every foul a penalty of 2 points is awarded to every player which gets included in score of his opponent.

Next player can play from any of the following places:

i. from in-hand,

ii. from where balls are in a dead position,

By doing anything out of following a player can commit a foul:

While striking:

i. out of turn;

ii. to ball other than cue-ball;

iii. when balls are in moving position;

iv. improperly from in-hand;

v. by both feet off the floor.

While attempting:

i. more than authorised hazards;

ii. a jump shot;

iii. more than 75 cannons;

iv. to use ball off the table;

v. a push stroke;

vi. to touch the ball with other part of cue than tip.

Spotting

(i) If no ball occupies the foot spot, balls which have to be spotted should be placed there. Balls should be placed in a straight line behind each other turn by turn if more than 1 ball is to be spotted. Line drawn from foot spot to bottom rail is known is Long String. Balls should be placed in line on long string, if multiple spotting of balls is necessary. Non spotted balls placed along long string line cannot be moved.

(ii) Balls which have been knocked from table or have pocketed in an illegal manner should be replaced on the table.

In following conditions balls should be spotted:

i. if in the same stroke in which cue ball is to pocketed, ball is made;

ii. if it is made in a stroke in which cue ball strike the designed object ball after striking anyother balls.

iii. if from the table ball is knocked;

Definitions

Match

Pre-determined number of games are included in a match.

Game

A game includes an agreed number of frames.

Striker

Person having right to strike the ball is called striker.

Balls

i. 15 red balls are used in the game;

ii. Ball of white colour is called cue-ball;

iii. Object balls have 6 colours.

Ball in Play

i. If ball is not in-hand, it is considered to have in play;

ii. If spotted, red should be considered to be in play. It

15

should remain so till potted or forced off the table;

Inspite of touching the ball with tip of cue, ball may not be considered to be in play if in opinion of refree player did not attempt to strike it.

Stroke

i. As soon as striker strikes the cue-ball with the help of tip of cue, striker is considered to hit the strike.

ii. A stroke which satisfies undermentioned conditions is considered to be a fair stroke:

a. Ball should be in a dead position at time of being striken and colours should be spotted properly;

b. Cue ball should not be strucked, but pushed.

c. Cue ball can be strucked only for one time in a single stroke.

d. At time of striking, striker should have either of his foot on floor.

forced off the table.

Stroke comes to an end as soon as ball comes in a dead position and striker leaves the table.

In following conditions ball is considered to be in-hand:

i. Ball is considered to be in-hand when it is out of the table;

ii. Until ball is played from in-hand or from here a foul is committed, it should considered to be in-hand;

iii. Ball is considered to be in-hand till turn of non-striker comes.

Jump Shot

Jump shot is a shot by which cue-ball jumps over anyother ball. However, when cue ball first strikes object ball and then jumps over another ball, this stroke should not be considered a jump shot.

Hazard

An hazard includes a pot or an in-off.

Occupied

If before touching another ball no ball has been placed on spot, it should be considered to have occupied.

Break

When strokes made in a turn are expressed in a series, it is known as a Break.

String

String is that state in which to leave the ball of player near to bottom cushion, together from Baulk-line to top cushion ball is played.

In-Off

After touching any object ball when cue-ball get into a pocket, it is termed in-off. However, it should be happened within rules.

Forced Off the Table

A ball is considered to be forced off the table if it does not comes in a dead position on any place other than bed of table or in the pocket.

Cannons

Cannon is a stroke in which cue-ball hit both object balls. However, it should be within rules of game.

Pot

Pot is a term which is used when ball without touching another ball enters into pocket. This should happened in accordance with rules.

Push Stroke

Tip of cue should not touch cue-ball while cue-ball touches object ball or when cue-ball has been commenced its forward motion. If this rule is overruled it is a foul which is known as Push-Stroke.

Equipments Used

Balls

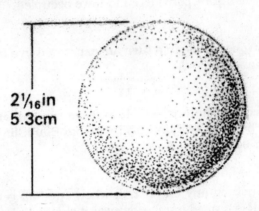

2¹/₁₆in
5.3cm

i. All balls should be of same weight. Balls of following weights are used in different events:

a. For Snooker Set balls of 3 gms;

b. For Billiard Set balls of 0.05 gms;

ii. Ball should have a radius of 26.25 mm and a tolerance capacity of 0.05 mm to 0.08mm.

Ancillary

For cue rests can be used to provide a bridge.

Cue

Cue should not a length of more than 910 mm. It should have a traditional accepted shape.

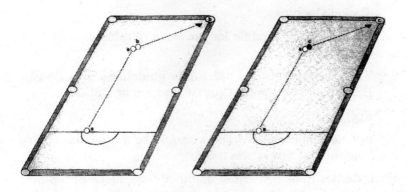

Billiard Table-Metric

The "D"

Bualk should have a semi-circle with a diameter of 584 mm. Centre of this semi-circle should be situated at middle of Baulk-line.

Pocket Openings

i. Corners and middle longer sides of table should have pockets.

ii. These pockets should fulfils guidelines provided by Billiards and Snooker Control Council or BSCC.

Spots

In following manner 4 spots should be marked on centre longitudinal line of the table:

i. Centre Spot : At equal distance from faces of top and bottom cushion and midway between centre pockets, this spot should be marked.

ii. Spot: At a distance of 320 mm from the perpendicular point below face of top cushion, this should be marked.

iii. In centre of Baulk-line one spot should mark.

iv. Pyramid Spot : Between centre spot and face of top cushion, this spot should be marked.

Height

From floor to top of cushion rail table should be situated at a height of about 850mm × 875mm.

Dimensions

Within the cushion faces playing area should have a size of 3500mm to 1750 mm. It should have a tolerance of ±3 mm on both dimension.

Baulk-line and Baulk

Line drawn parallel to bottom cushion at a distance of 700 m from it is known as Baulk-Line, whereas intervening space is know as the Baulk.

Table of Billiard-Imperial

Height

From floor to top of the cushion rail table should be

situated at a height of 2ft $9^{1/2}$ ins × 2 ft $10^{1/2}$ ins.

Pocket Openings

i. Corner and middle of longer side should have pockets;

ii. These pockets should fulfils guidelines of BSCC.

Dimensions

Within cushion faces playing area should have a size of 11 ft. 8^{12} ins × 5 ft 10 ins, and a tolerance of ±0.5 on both dimensions.

Spots

In following manner 4 spots should be marked on centre of longitudinal line of table:

i. In centre of Baulk-line;

ii. Spot : Below face of top cushion at a distance of $12^{3/4}$ from perpendicular point.

iii. Centre Spot : At equal distance from faces of top and bottom cushion and midway between centre pockets this spot should be marked.

iv. Pyramid Spot: Midway between centre spot and face of top cushion this spot should be marked.

Rules of Rotation

With following exceptions rules of Pocket Billiard applies in this game:

Purpose of the Game

Balls should be pocketed in a numerical order from 1 to 15. Players receive points according to numerical order of balls, or in other words for hitting balls of higher designation players will receive higher points.

Player scoring 61 points is declare winner of the game.

Starting the Game

i. On break 1-ball should be the object ball. For pocketed

balls to count this ball should be strucked first.

ii. 1-ball should be placed at apex of a rack of triangular shaped in such a way that on left-hand-corner 2 balls are placed and on right-hand corner 3-ball situates. Other balls should positioned randomly in the rack.

Uninterrupted Play

i. Any ball which is pocketed in an illegal stroke should be spotted;

ii. All balls which have been pocketed in a legal stroke should be taken into consideration;

iii. To ensure the balls are to be played according to their numerical order, object ball for each shot is established. Before striking anyother ball, ball having lowest number should be strucked by cue ball.

Continuous Pocket Billiards

Basic rules of Pocket Billard applies in this game with the following exceptions:

Starting the Game

15-numbered object balls should be racked in a triangle at foot of table in such a way that 15-ball is placed at apex and on the foot spot.

On rear left-hand corner of the triangle 1-ball should be placed and on rear right-hand corner 5-ball should be placed. At bottom of triangle lower numbered balls while at top of it higher numbered balls should be placed.

Non-Interrupted Play

a. On every shot shooter can opt:

i. to strike the called ball and another object ball which knocked the second ball into a cushion or pocket,

ii. to rail with cue ball after striking the called ball;

iii. to pocket the called ball.

BILLIARDS RULE BOOK

Penalties

a. Player can loose his turn and a penalty of 1 point can be awarded for a scratch;

b. A penalty of additional 15 points should be awarded for three succeeding scratches by the player.

Rules of 8-Ball Game

With following exceptions basic rules of pocket billiard apply in this game:

Starting the Game
a. Shooter can choose high or low numbered balls as his object balls, if balls have been pocketed on the break. This option will transfer to other player if first player does not pocket the ball on break. Till ball is pocketed final designation of object balls should not be assigned.

b. On the break atleast one object ball should be driven.

c. Balls should be racked in such a way that 8-ball is placed in centre of third row from front apex of rack.

d. If any shooter pocketed the 8-ball on break, he should be declared winner of game.

Purpose of Game

Basic aim of every player is to pocket the 8-ball first. Balls numbered from 1 to 7 are object balls for one player and balls numbered from 9 to 15 are object balls for other player.

8-ball is not allowed to be pocketed, however on break till designated balls have been pocketed, it can be pocketed.

Non-Interrupted Play

a. A shot will be considered to be legal if shooter contact his own ball first Combinations balls having any ball are allowed.

23

b. If any shooter pocketed his opponent's ball, advantage of this should be enjoyed by opponent.

c. 8-ball should be pocketed after all designated balls have been pocketed.

d. A shot at 8-ball will be considered to be legal if that shooter call the pocket into which ball will fall and 8-ball should be strucked first.

Penalties

A player can loose the game if he commit any of the following errors:

i. Pocket the 8-ball before it becomes object ball;

ii. 8-ball is pocketed in pocket in place of that called by shooter;

iii. Neither cue-ball nor 8-ball contact a rail in flailing to make 8-ball;

iv. While 8-ball is pocketed scratch occurs.

Players

Absence

If any player cannot be present in room, he can appoint his substitute.

Unfair Conduct

A player can lose a game if:

He refuse to continue a frame;

Behaves in an unfair manner.

For above mentioned behaviour a player can be disqualified from the game in competitions which are held under control of Billiards and Snooker Council or its Affiliated Associations.

Time Wasting

A player will be warned and can be disqualified if refree

thinks that he is taking a lot of time in playing the stroke.

Non-Striker

While striker is playing his stroke other player is not allowed to stand or move in line of sight. It is done with a view to avoid every kind of disturbance to strike.

Officials of Game

The Marker

Marker is required to keep the score on marking board and to help refree in perform his duties.

The Referee

Main duties of refree includes the following:

a. He should ensure that game is being played in accordance with basic rules;

b. He should discontinuity the play if there is any breach of rule;

c. He will tell colour of ball if player has a problem in seeing the colours properly;

d. On the request of player he has to clean the ball.

He should ignore any question which is not stated by rules;

He is not require to indicate to any player that he may commit a foul.

RULES OF SNOOKER

Game

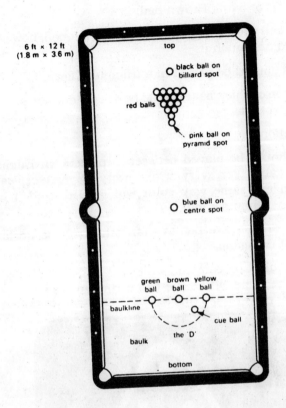

Location of Balls

At starting of each frame object balls should be placed in the following way:

On pyramid spot Pink ball;

On left-hand Green ball;

On the spot Black ball;

On centre spot Blue ball;

On right-hand correct of D Yellow ball;

On middle of baulk Brown ball;

At apex ball should be placed nearer to Pink ball, however, it should not touch it;

Red ball should be placed in a triangular form;

Near to top cushion base should be designed which should be parallel to it.

Explanation

Game should be played between 2 players on English Billiard Table. For every stroke every player receives a point, in the same way point will be deducted if his opponent commits a foul.

Player scoring more points than other will be declare winner of the game.

There should be a common white cue-ball and 21 object balls in the game. White cue-ball is common in the sense that every player uses this ball.

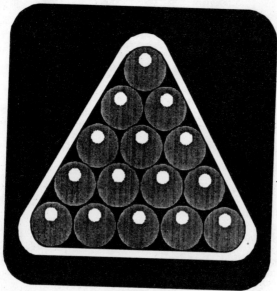

15 reds with 1 value and of following colours with different values should be there:

Blue has a value of 5;

Green has a value of 3;

Brown has a value of 4;

Yellow has a value of 2;

Black valued 7;

Pink valued 6.

Till all reds are off the table scoring strokes can be made by potting the reds and after that by potting colours having less value first and more value later.

Play from in hand

Play will be considered from in-hand when cue-ball has been strucked from on or within lines of D.

How to Play

i. Players are required to decide the order in which they will play. It should be kept in mind that this order cannot be changed during the play.

ii. First player will play from in-hand and with first stroke frame is considered to have began.

iii. At beginning of game cue ball should first hit a ball and should not be in the pocket.

iv. Only ball on must can enter into pocket.

v. (a) At beginning of each turn red should be considered the Ball On;

(b) Value of red which have been potted in a single stroke is scored.

vi. If Red has been potted, such ball should be potted

next which can be scored from being potted. Ball of this colour should be spotted again.

vii. Only Red and colours should be potted turn-by-turn to continue the break till all Reds are off the table;

viii. If striker was unable to score any point, right to strike passes to other player, who has to play from where cue-ball came into rest.

ix. Balls should be used in ascending order of their value, in other words, balls of higher value should be used first and then balls of lower value.

x. If score of both player is not equal and only Black balls have been left out with first score or foul frame will come to an end:

a. To decide order of play, a lot should be drawn;

b. Ball of black colour should be spotted;

c. Frame will come to an end with other score or foul;

d. Coming player should begin from in-hand.

Hitting of More than One Ball in Same Stroke

A player can hit only 1 ball in a single stroke. However, he can hit 2 reds or a free ball.

Spotting Colours

i. If a colour whose own spot has been occupied is to be spotted, it should be placed on highest value;

ii. If balls of different colours have to be spotted and their own spots have been already occupied, ball of highest value should be spotted first;

iii. If no spot is empty, colour should be placed near to its own spot between that spot and nearest part of top cushion, however, if in Black and Pink there is no space between its own spot and nearest part of top cushion, colour should be placed near to its own spot on centre line of table below that spot.

Ball On

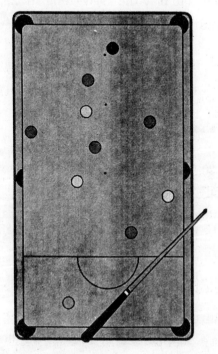

It is same as mentioned earlier.

Ball on Edge of Pocket

i. A ball should be placed again on the table if it has fallen into pocket without hitting another ball;

ii. All balls on table have to replaced if striked ball has touched it. In this condition striker will get an opportunity to play his stroke again.

iii. Ball which balances on edge and falls in should not be replaced.

Ball without Obstruction

i. Refree should state Free Ball if cue-ball is snookered

after a foul;

ii. Any ball can be considered As On by Non-Offending player if he has to play the succeeding stroke;

iii. For this purpose, free ball will be considered to be Ball On;

iv. If cue-ball is not hit first, it is consider a foul;

v. If free ball is to be potted it should be spotted, and value of ball on should be scored;

vi. Ball On should be scored if it is potted;

vii. In condition when both Free ball as well as Ball On are potted, value of ball On should be scored only.

Touching ball

Refree will state Touching Ball if any ball or ball which is or going to be On is being touched by Cue-Ball.

Penalties

For the following fouls a penalty of 4 points should be awarded:

Through Causing

a. If there is a push stroke, or in other words if there is any foul.

b. It enters a pocket.

c. If cue ball does hit a ball on,

d. If a ball is forced off the table.

e. If ball not correctly spotted was striken.

f. If ball is touched with not tip of cue but from anywhere else.

Through Unfair Stroke:

a. If strikes improperly from in hand.

b. If at time of striking no feet was on the floor.

c. If player strikes more than once in same stroke.

d. If player strikes without his turn.

By causing

a. If it enters a pocket.

b. If cue-ball does not hit a ball on.

c. If cue ball first strikes object ball and then jumps over any other ball.

d. If player snooker with free ball.

If striker uses a ball which is off the table or uses as the cue ball any ball other than white or after potting a red commits a foul before nominating a colour, a penalty of 7 points should be awarded for this foul.

Fouls

In relation to fouls following things should be kept in mind:

a. As soon as any player commits a foul, refree should call loudly Foul and after completion of stroke should announce penalty;

b. Before beginning of next stroke it should be ignored if neither refree has awarded it nor non-player has demanded it;

c. Ball which have been positioned improperly should not be touched and replaced properly, however, if it off the table, it should be replaced;

d. All points scored before awarding of fouls are permissible;

e. Next stroke should be made from place where cue-ball stopped moving.

A player who committed more than 1 foul in a single stroke should be awarded a penalty of higher value.

Ball moved by other than striker

Refree will replace the ball again if it was disturbed by anybody other than striker.

Stalemate

If refree thinks that striker can approach Stalement, he should be warned to change the situation. If he does not change this position, his frame can be declared null and void, and can be ordered to start again.

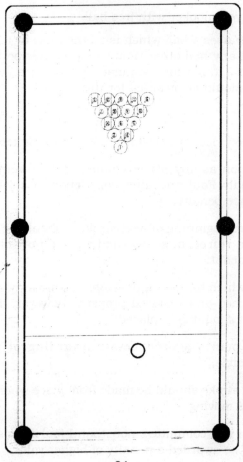

BILLIARDS RULE BOOK

Rules of Four Handed Snooker

i. Players will determine order in which they have to play at beginning of game. This order should not be changed throughout the game. Each side will open different frames alternately.

ii. Although, order of play should not be changed, but if player wants they can do so only at beginning of a fame.

iii. Player committing a foul will play again, but order of play will not change.

iv. In this game a player can talk with his partner when striker is off the table.

Meaning of Important Concepts

Nominated ball

Ball which a striker indicates to refree that he will hit with first impact of cue-ball is known as Nominated Ball.

Break

i. Next stroke will be strucked by same player if ball is forced off the table;

ii. In one turn number of pots made in succession are termed as break.

Ball on

Ball to which cue-ball hit first is known as Ball On.

Pot

i. When after contacting with other ball an object ball enters a pocket, a pot is considered;

Snookered

i. When a direct stroke in a straight line to any part of every ball on is obstructed by a ball or balls not on, cue-ball is considered to be Snookered;

ii. Cue-ball can be obstructed only if it is obstructed from all positions on or within lines of D;

iii. Ball near to cue-ball should be considered the snookering ball if cue-ball is obstructed by more than one ball.

Angled

i. When corner of the cushion obstructs a direct stroke in a straight line to any part of every Ball On, cue-ball is considered to be angled;

ii. Refree is required to call Angled Ball;

iii. Striker can play it from in-hand, if he wants.

Foul

If any player does not follow the rules of game properly, it is considered to be a foul.

Officials

Marker

Marker will keep score on marking board and will help refree in performing his duty properly.

Referee

Location of Referee

Refree is the sole judge of play and his decisions are binding on everybody.

Duties of Refree includes the following:

i. If requested he should clean the ball.

ii. It is his duty to stop the play if he observers breach of any rule.

iii. He should tell colour of ball if player has problem of colour blindness.

It is to be kept in mind that a referee is not required to answer any question regarding differences in scores.

BILLIARDS RULE BOOK

Brief Description of Important Concepts Used in Billiards and Snooker

Table: It is a slate bed, covered with green baize having dimensions of the standard size table. Basically it should have the following things:

cushion of 2in width, centre pocket of 3½ in width, top pocket of 2in width, spot, centre spot, pyramid spot, balk line, the D, long butt cue, half butt cue.

There should be sufficient lighting in order to avoid any kind of disturbance.

Start: The red ball is placed on the spot, and the striker places his cue ball at any point in the D and plays the first shot. When his turn ended, the second player brings his cue ball into play.

Duration: Play lasts an agreed length of time, or until one player or side reaches an agreed number of points.

Balls: The white and spot white are the cue balls, one used by each player.

Balls touching: If the striker's ball comes to rest against another ball, the red ball is replaced on the spot.

Distraction: The non-striker must not do anything to distract the striker.

Making a Shot: The striker uses the tip of his cue to hit his cue ball in the direction of another ball.

Fouls: A striker who makes any foul shot loses his turn and any score he has made in that break. In addition, he concedes points to his opponents in certain cases.

Scoring: The striker scores points for winning hazards, losing hazards, and cannons. All points accumulated in a shot are counted.

Snooker

This game is played on a pocket billard table. 15 red, 6

coloured, and one white cue ball are used. It may be played by two persons, pairs, or teams.

Starting Play: A coin is tossed to decide who will play first. The game begins with the starter playing the cue ball from within the D at any red ball.

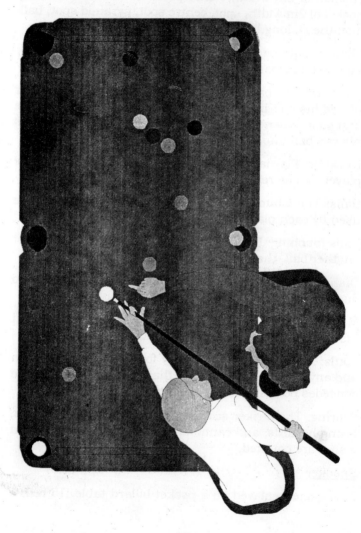

Duration: The player with the highest score when all balls are cleared from the table is winner. When only the last ball is left, the first score or penalty ends the game unless this makes the scores equal.

Table: It is played on any standard pocket billard table.

Rules: The initial stroke of each turn must strike the cue ball against a red, so long as any red remains on the table. If the striker succeeds in pocketing a red, he scores that ball and continues his break by attempting to pocket any non-red ball.

Red balls that are pocketed are not replaced on the table; but coloured balls are immediately re-spotted.

Play continues until there are no red balls left on the table. The player pocketing the last red may attempt to pocket any coloured ball. If he succeeds, that coloured ball is re-spotted. After this the coloured balls must be struck by the cue ball.

Snooker: A player is snookered when a ball he must not play obstructs a straight line between the cue ball and the ball that is on. He must attempt his shot, and will be penalized for missing the on ball or first hitting any other ball.

Fouls: After any foul shot, the striker loses his turn and any score that he may have made on that break. His opponent receives the appropriate penalty score, and has the option of playing the balls where they have come to rest or of asking the other player to do so.